# The Mickey Mouse Club Scrapbook

compiled by Keith Keller

Grosset & Dunlap • Publishers • New York

# Acknowledgments

I would like to extend my warm thanks to the many employees of Walt Disney Productions and Grosset & Dunlap without whose efforts and talents this book could not have been completed: to Dave Smith, Disney Studio archivist, for his advice, personal interest, and dedication to detail; to Dave Spencer and the Disney Studio still camera department for their tremendous help in compiling the pictures; to Gary Graf for aid in drafting the manuscript; to Karen Prindle, for the proverbial "little things" (including an abundance of typing); and to Howard Ashman, my editor at Grosset.

Special thanks also to the Mouseketeers themselves, whose kind cooperation and personal involvement were invaluable — and especially to my pal, the Big Mooseketeer, Roy Williams, who provided many insights.

To my mother Eunice, my brother Kerry, my sister Karen, and my lovingly remembered father Raymond, another round of heartfelt thanks. I cannot express the feelings I hold for each of you.

Love and enthusiasm were synonymous with the Mickey Mouse Club. The same has been true of this project.

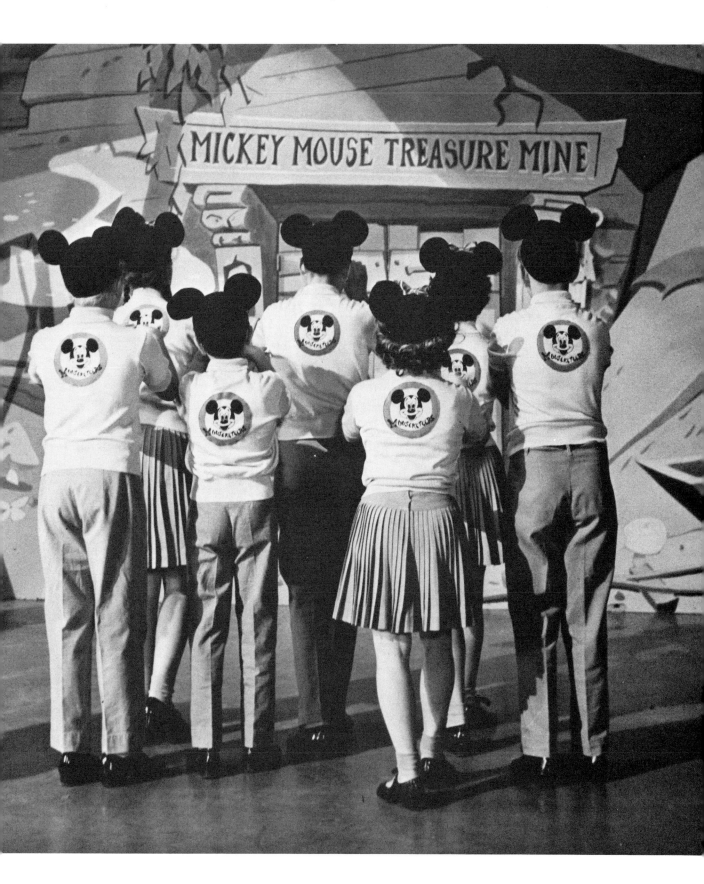

# Contents

# Author's Note

We fought like crazy over the television set: my brother (younger), my sister (older), my mother, and me. The force and scope of our video battles rage in my childhood memories—reducing Little League baseball, kick-the-can, and backyard barbecues to minor souvenirs of the Fabulous Fifties. My father finally had to mediate: he allotted Sunday afternoons to Mom, and the rest of the week he divided up among the three of us. Each kid got two days of viewing autonomy.

We didn't agree on much back then—our differences in age and sex saw to that. In fact, in 1955–56 and 1956–57 we only agreed for one hour every weekday. We agreed that we ought to watch the Mickey Mouse Club. In 1957–58 and 1958–59, the Disney people cut the show back to one-half hour. (I later learned they did it because of production difficulties.) I doubt if they ever knew that they'd cut my family's peace and quiet back to one-half hour a day as well.

I sang along. I wore my ears. I hoped that Donald would get the best of the gong. Spin and Marty were my personal pals and, at seven years old, I loved Annette.

And I wasn't the only one. Ten million kids felt exactly the same from 5:00 to 6:00 P.M. in 1955. The show is twenty years old this year and marches along in syndication. It's been seen in eighteen foreign countries. It ran for nine years in France alone.

This is a book about why and when and how the whole thing happened. It's pictures, mostly, and songs, and a unique show business story. But most of all, it's a scrapbook to remind myself and everyone else who cares at all how wonderful it was to be an honorary Mouseketeer.

1.

2.

5.

6.

9.

10.

3.

4.

7.

8.

11.

12.

# The Leaders of the Club

The story of the Mickey Mouse Club is best told in the words of some of the people who made it come to pass. Bill Walsh was the show's producer. Here's how he says it all began.

**Walsh:** *I guess it all started back around 1949.*

*Television was still regarded as something like going to the moon. You can't imagine what it was like then. People couldn't conceive of pictures — real pictures — going through the air. The radio folks laughed themselves silly and kept on going.*

*Everybody laughed like crazy at the Television Academy, across the street from the Hollywood Athletic Club on Sunset Boulevard in a building owned by Edgar Bergen. Edgar, I believe, was one of the Academy's first presidents, mainly because he owned the building. Programming itself consisted of roller derby, a lot of wrestling, and a little Milton Berle. So it makes sense that Walt originally became interested in TV not as an entertainment medium, but as a device to sell theatrical products — feature films.*

*From the onset of television, we were approached by the networks because they assumed that Disney, a very visual person, could be helpful to them. But Walt didn't cotton right away to their suggestions.*

Disney's first essay into television reflected his view of the new medium as a promotional device. The show, a Christmas special, was a glorified trailer for *Alice in Wonderland,* the feature film scheduled for release in the summer of 1951. What actually enticed Disney into television at all is somewhat of a mystery.

**Walsh:** *An agency man from St. Louis appeared on the scene, a salesman-type fellow, who thought it would be useful to get Walt involved in the new medium. He had an essay written on what television really* was. *Because at that time nobody knew what it was. I mean literally, nobody knew what the heck it was. The essay helped convince Walt that he should do a Christmas show and do it on TV. And that's what he did.*

Prior to coming to work for Walt Disney Productions, Bill Walsh had spent half of his life in show business. Educated at the University of Missouri, he had been variously employed as a radio scriptwriter, reporter, columnist, and press agent. It was fresh from fifteen years of press agentry with the Ettinger Company that Walsh came to Disney. He said he hadn't the faintest idea of why Disney selected him to produce the first television venture.

*Bill Walsh, who produced the Mickey Mouse Club during its entire three years of live filming (1955–57). When the club went off the air, he turned his attention to feature films — Mary Poppins, The Absent-minded Professor, and Bedknobs and Broomsticks among others. This picture was taken in 1970.*

**Walsh:** *I kept bumping into him in the hall, which is not a bad place, or in the parking lot. He used to wonder who is that funny looking fellow, because I was a press agent in those days, as you know, and not a very good one. And then one day, in his strange way, he said, "You, you be the producer of TV." And I said, "Huh? I don't have any experience as a producer." And Walt said (he would always say), "Who does?"*

"One Hour in Wonderland" was aired on NBC on December 25, 1950. Besides the major film sequences from *Alice*, the show featured clips from other theatrical films and an appearance by Edgar Bergen and Charlie McCarthy, whom Walsh had brought to the studio in 1946 to narrate *Mickey and the Beanstalk*, an animated short. "One Hour in Wonderland" also featured an appearance by Mr. Disney himself, with his daughters Sharon and Diane, in a set designed to recreate Disney's studio office. The "office set" came to be a mainstay of the Disney television format for years to come; Walt would take a book from the shelf of his warm, homey office to introduce the evening's entertainment with a sincerely personal touch. "One Hour in Wonderland" was sponsored by Coca-Cola.

The next day, the show evoked an enthusiastic response from the Tele Review column of *Daily Variety:*

---

*Hollywood's first picture produced by a major studio for television, and budgeted far beyond any previous videopus was spread across the nation yesterday at 4:00 P.M. to top off a day of festive joy for the youngsters. That it played to perhaps the biggest audience in TV history must be conceded, but more importantly it proved what can be done with skilled integration of cartoon characters and live subjects with the end result superb entertainment.*

*The inkwell imps of Walt Disney were here making their debut on the channels with the little wooden men of Edgar Bergen to the undoubted delight of millions of youngsters and elders as well. High fun in fantasy and comedy, it skipped along blithely through the fastest hour in television. Both Disney and Bergen played themselves and deployed their characters like toy soldiers on the living room floor. No prompting of audience laughs was needed to keep the hilarity rolling. It exploded the fallacy of comedy producers that live reaction is a necessary adjunct to filming.*

*Through the device of Disney's magic mirror, with Hans Conried as the eerie figure bringing to life for the youngsters, including Disney's two daughters, highlights from past cartoon classics, was unfolded footage from such standouts as* Snow White, Song of the South, Uncle Remus, *Donald Duck, Mickey, Pluto, Goofy and a preview of the mad tea party from Disney's forthcoming* Alice in Wonderland. *In the live section were the Firehouse Five Plus Two, Bobby Driscoll and Kathryn Beaumont.*

---

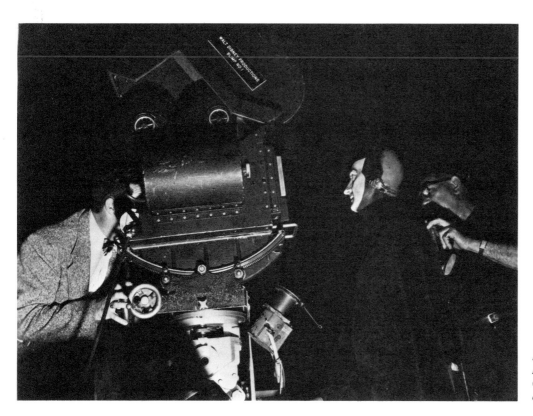

*Hans Conried, as the Magic Mirror, before the Christmas Special cameras.*

*The Magic Mirror as he appeared to television and studio audiences on "One Hour in Wonderland," Walt Disney's first television venture — on Christmas Day, 1950.*

The first Christmas special's marked success prompted an encore the following year on CBS. "The Walt Disney Christmas Show" was aired on December 25, 1951.

**Walsh:** *This time, we went on for Johnson and Johnson, the finest name in surgical dressings, and it was essentially the same thing—snatches of pictures here and there. This was what Walt originally conceived — a device to sell pictures. In fact, the other studios were beginning to snarl at him for getting all this marvelous free space. They hadn't figured it out yet. Instead, they were wrapped up in creating series for themselves which would pay them back in money. I don't think Walt ever cottoned to making money off TV. He'd only wanted to use it to sell pictures. So we had two Christmas shows under our belts at this time. Now the nibbles came from the networks, right? TV was, by now, really burgeoning and the joint was jumping.*

But two other things were also burgeoning in the early 1950s. The first was Disney's dream: a theme park in Anaheim, California, which would shortly take the official title Disneyland. The second was the dream of a local Hollywood television station to become a third network, the American Broadcasting Corporation.

**Walsh:** *In those days, a third network was like a third political party, and ABC was looking for a way to put itself on the map with a dramatic flourish. They came to Walt to suggest that they would put money into the theme fest at Disneyland. Neither NBC nor CBS was willing to come up with much scratch for the park, so ABC won exclusive television rights to Disney productions in return for a major investment.*

A weekly variety series was planned and hatched, largely as a vehicle to promote not only films and merchandise featuring Disney characters, but also the park itself. It was from "The Magic Kingdom," Disneyland, that the series took its title and the first episode, "The Disneyland Story," introduced millions of viewers to the soon-to-be-opened playground. The show premiered on October 27, 1954. With Bill Walsh at the production helm, the series rocketed from tenth to second place in the ratings, during

*Sleeping Beauty's castle under construction at Disneyland.*

its first four months on the air. On December 15, 1954, a new element entered the "Disneyland" format — the serialized adventures of Davy Crockett.

**Walsh:** *We wanted a series about legendary Americans, and the first one we happened to pick on was, accidentally, Davy Crockett. Walt wasn't too thrilled at first. We did storyboards and threw in everything but the kitchen sink: fighting Indians, tomahawk duels with Seminoles down in Florida, Crockett going to Congress and fighting Andy Jackson, adventures out West, early Texans, and, finally, the battle for the Alamo, with Davy dying as he had lived — swinging his rifle around with a pile of seventeen dead enemies in front of him. Walt heard all of this and said, I'll never forget this, "Yeah, but what does he* do?"

No need to take time here to talk about the marketing of coonskin caps; "Davy Crockett" was a runaway hit, clinching the success of "Disneyland's" first season.

**Walsh:** *Now, there was a lot of action in New York from the network. Walt called me in one day, and I asked if we were going to be renewed for another year. He said, "We think so, it's going very well." So I said, "Good, 'cause I'm getting tired. I'd like to go on vacation now." And Walt said, "Wait a minute, wait a minute, I have something to discuss with you . . ." I said, "Boy, you know I didn't think we'd get through that first year. We were used to doing an hour every three to five years for animation, but doing a show every week, that was murder." Walt said, "Yes, yes." I said, "What's the idea?" And he said, "An hour every day."*
*    "An hour every day?"*
*    "Yes — with children."*

And so, the Mickey Mouse Club was born. Disney's original concept for the show had its roots in the Mickey Mouse Clubs which Harry W. Woodin and the Disney studio had organized in the 1930s. These clubs, designed to draw children into movie theatres, held "meetings" at Saturday matinees. They featured sing-alongs, birthday celebrations, and installation of club officers (including a "Chief Mickey Mouse" and a "Chief Minnie Mouse") who were selected from children in the audience. By 1932, Mickey Mouse Clubs had over one million members across the United States. By 1935, the clubs had proven too unwieldy and most disbanded. At least one, however — Sonny Shepherd's Mickey Mouse Club in Miami, Florida — persisted into the 1950s.

*Bill Walsh before a Mickey Mouse Club storyboard (1955). Wednesday is called Stunt Night (left, middle) here. It will later be dubbed Anything Can Happen Day.*

16

## The Original
## Mickey Mouse Club
## (1929–1933)

*A poster (right) for the Mickey Mouse Clubs that sprang up in movie theaters across the country from 1929–1933.*

*"Currency" (below) of the Mickey Mouse Club of Phoenix, Arizona. The clubs pulled children into the theaters for Saturday matinees.*

*"Minnie's Yoo Hoo," the Mickey Mouse theme music that became a fad song of the 1930s, was fitted with special club lyrics. Sing-along film was supplied to the theaters by Disney.*

# OFFICIAL BULLETIN
## — OF THE —
# MICKEY MOUSE CLUB

LUCILLE ALLEN BENEDICT
General Manager

Walt Disney Productions, Ltd.    2719 Hyperion Ave., Hollywood

| Volume II | HOLLYWOOD, CALIFORNIA, JULY 15, 1932 | Number 13 |

# Unusual Show Draws Crowds at Miami

## "Wedding Party of Mickey Mouse" Basis of Splendid Entertainment By Mickey Mouse Club

Coming to the front again with an unusual idea, Sonny Shepherd, Manager of the Biltmore Theatre at Miami, Florida, packed them in at four performances of a Mickey Mouse Show at a downtown theatre.

Photographs of the show and newspaper stories crediting Mr. Shepherd with staging the finest kid show ever to reach Miami, were the rewards reaped by this energetic showman for his efforts.

Mr. Shepherd has sent us a (Continued on page 3)

## "Card Toss" Interesting Game

A good hot-weather contest which provides lots of fun with a minimum of exertion on the part of the contestants, is a "Card Toss."

Stretch a line across one end of the stage, about six feet from the ground.

Contestants are placed in back of a designated mark on the floor, about three feet from the line. Each contestant is given an equal number of cards, preferably with different colored backs in order to avoid disputes.

The object of the game is to toss the cards over the line, the child throwing most over the line winning.

A variation of this game is called "In Your Hat." However, this necessitates a supply of hats of some kind, preferably a (Continued on page 3)

SCENE FROM SUCCESSFUL STAGE SHOW, "THE WEDDING OF MICKEY MOUSE," PRESENTED AT MIAMI

*The bimonthly bulletin circulated from the California headquarters to clubs across the nation.*

Disney seems to have had these clubs in mind when he first presented Walsh with the idea of a daily television program with the same title. In the following notes, made by Disney on December 8, 1954, the "mouse party," "song slide," and audience participation suggestions all hark back to Woodin's original clubs. The idea of selecting children from a studio audience to play Mickey, Donald, and other characters is obviously based on the old "Chief Mickey" idea.

---

**Mickey Mouse Club Show**
**Suggestions by Walt—December 8, 1954**

*Mouse party: audience participation*

*Children selected to be Mickey, Donald, etc.*
  *(with costumes), others play the part of Pluto, cat, etc.*

*Children from audience visit with characters from history*

*Special shows acted by children in Disneyland*

*Presents to kinds in audience with birthdays,*
  *also unbirthday presents*

*Drawing lessons*

*Gadget band: kids participate*

*Animal acts*

*Magician*

*Story of children around the world, children in sports*
  *(honor Sunday school teachers?)*

*Everyone Can Sing: song slides*

---

By late January, 1955, Bill Walsh was ready to present a much amplified outline based on Disney's suggestions:

**The Mickey Mouse Club**
**Children's TV Show**
**General Format Notes and Preliminary Structure**
**by Bill Walsh**

*As a starting point, and for general purposes of discussion, a preliminary structure for the Mickey Mouse Club, an hourly daily children's TV program, has been set up in the following notes.*

*1. By its intent and nature, the Mickey Mouse Club is planned to attract and hold the greatest available children's audience between the ages of three and fourteen, between the hours of 5:00 and 6:00 P.M. Monday through Friday nights.*

*2. Because of our basic ingredients, the names of Walt Disney and Mickey Mouse, the children will expect, and should receive, a substantial measure of cartoon entertainment during the week's shows.*

  *I believe we should make reasonably frequent use of these shorts,*

KID SHOW —
MICKEY MOUSE
— CLUB —

CLUB HOUSE AT
DISNEY LAND —
ENTER CLUB THRU
CAVE — UP HOLLOW
TREE TO TREE HOUSE
PARABLE OF
THE TALENTS —

CONTESTS —
PRIZES —

RE INACT FAMOUS
EVENTS IN HISTORY
WITH CLUB MEMBERS
ENACTING ROLES —

MEMBERS SUGEST
IDEAS FOR CLUB
HOUSE —

FAMOUS MEN SUGEST
IDEAS FOR CLUB
RE-EISENHOWER

CLUB SONG —

OUT STANDING
CLUB TALENT TO
GO ON DISNEYLAND
SHOW —

TOUR COUNTRY
WITH CLUB
SHOW —

*From the desk of Mr. Disney: random notes on the club (left), dated summer, 1954. They represent the first evidence of a television Mickey Mouse Club brewing in the back of Walt's mind. Not quite a year later, he sent an official memo (below) giving sanction to the name "Mouseketeer." Tom Moore, the Roving Mouseketeer, was cut from the format before the premiere.*

WALT DISNEY PRODUCTIONS

WALT DISNEY

INTER-OFFICE COMMUNICATION

P-139

TO HAL ADELQUIST           DATE APRIL 15, 1955

FROM WALT DISNEY           SUBJECT

The talented kids on the Mickey Mouse Club Show will be called MOUSEKETEERS, while the adults will be known as MOOSEKETEERS — for example, Roy Williams will be called the BIG MOOSEKETEER. Jimmy Dodd will be the MUSICAL MOOSEKETEER. Tom Moore will be called the ROVING MOOSEKETEER. This will give them a chance to do a lot of things with Moore. He can show up anywhere from Siam to the Flying Carpet. Damiani will be the MAESTRO. George Bruns and his group will be known as the MICKEY MOUSE CLUB BAND.

The younger, less talented kids, who are still amateurs, are to be called MEESKETEERS.

All three categories can be broken down into sub-divisions. Also, on occasion, they will have honorary guests in each of the three groups.


cc: Bill Walsh
    Bill Anderson

during the early months of the program; then, as our audience is attracted and solidified, we can start tapering off a bit.

3. However, to give the illusion of a lot of cartoon on the show, I believe we should have certain standard sections of animated footage used on all shows as a definite Disney trademark. This regular footage would be used in the opening, the program identification, the Mickey Mouse Club song, possibly the installation of officers' song, and the sign-off song.

4. Each hour show is divided into four fifteen-minute segments. This appears to be advantageous, both from the multiple sponsors' viewpoint and from our own.

The segments should be set up so that they are, in most cases, interchangeable with one another, and can be fitted into other shows on a rerun schedule.

5. The children. It is apparent, even at this early date, that children, in addition to being our audience, will also constitute a considerable part of our show as performers.

In many cases, these children will be selected directly from the audience. However, in conversation with experienced hands on audience participation shows, they make it clear that for certain purposes, audience participants should be screened beforehand.

This should be done for such routines as panel quizzes, stunts, or any bit where the assured reaction and cooperation of the contestant becomes a vital part of the success of the event.

In some cases, it will be necessary to engage in pre-planning with the children's parents or teachers to produce a desired effect.

6. Guest Stars. In general, our guest stars will be drawn from many worlds besides the field of entertainment. They may be athletes, heroes, doctors, naturalists, scientists, or collectors. However, the format can easily encompass such guests as Roy Rogers, Bergen and McCarthy, Red Skelton, Ed Wynn, or anyone who may become available to us on a reasonable basis.

7. Scenery, Costumes, Props. In keeping with Disney tradition, I believe our scenery, costumes, and props should all be given overall style, good taste, and capable of evoking the utmost in imagination and fun. The sets can be imaginative and fun, without being elaborate. With an audience of imaginative children, sometimes a couple of props and a few lines on a backdrop can produce a beautiful castle for Sleeping Beauty.

8. Exploitation. As in the parent Disneyland show; proper exploitation of Disney films and merchandise becomes a basic part of our structure.

In the additional leeway possible on a children's show, we can work picture exploitation into children's games and contests throughout the entertainment section of the show.

As an example, take The Littlest Outlaw, a virtually unknown motion picture title. We can take over the job of building it into a known title. . . .

9. Film. Because motion picture film is to play such a large and variegated part in the Mickey Mouse Club, it is well to give our special

needs in this department early consideration. It will be necessary, of course, to arrange or set up proper production units, here and elsewhere, to get this film planned and into work. . . .

10. *The Mickey Mouse Club* Cast. *The selection of the Mickey Mouse Stock Company—the people who will conduct the Mickey Mouse show on stage from day to day—is of course a vital consideration, and should receive an extended period of screening, auditioning, and a process of trial and error.*

*The regular Disney cartoon characters will turn up on screen frequently to bulwark this stock company and give the proceedings an unmistakable Disney flavor.*

*In our search for Mickey Mouse Club performers, it will be our job to find individuals who best bridge the gap from Disney cartoons to live people in a manner that is believable and entertaining.*

*For discussion purposes and as a point of departure, a cast structure has been set forth in the following.*

*It is recognized that, as time goes by, our ideas on these cast characters may undergo considerable change. We have given each of them temporary names:*

*Smee, the program conductor or general master of ceremonies. He should have an eccentric makeup and costume. (Basically, one that conceals his own human personality). It is his job to coordinate all phases of the program for the audience.*

*Mary Lee, the girl member of the company. She should be pretty, friendly, completely relaxed in the Betty White or Fran Allison tradition. Mothers and children should like her immediately. Fathers too in a pinch. She should sing, be able to tell a story, conduct semiserious panels, and serve as a friendly beacon and confidant for little girls who come up onto the stage.*

*A Genie, the Mickey Mouse Club official magician. He lives in a bottle or lamp (trick photography) and appears frequently enough to probably justify his inclusion as a regular member of the staff.*

*Ellsworth, a Talking Mynah Bird, a mechanical or hand puppet bird personality who hangs out in a cage or stage box near the proscenium arch. Ellsworth is an impudent, Charlie McCarthy type of personality who makes rude remarks about the proceedings from time to time.*

*Animal Crackers Orchestra, a group of six musicians and a leader with a large range of flexibility. They should wear costumes, double and triple on instruments, and a few should be able to sing or perform in novelty numbers. Basically a gadget band, they should none the less be able to convey sentimental moods when the occasion rises.*

11. *The following format is a mock-up of a week's Monday to Friday programming. Each night falls into a general category, in this way:*

*Monday—Travel Night*
*Tuesday—Participation and Improvement*
*Wednesday—Musical Night*

# MOUSEKA-DICTIONARY

### with mousekedefinitions

| | | |
|---|---|---|
| **MOUSEKETEER**<br>Boy or girl | **MEESEKETEER**<br>Very little boy,<br>or very little girl | **BIG MOOSEKETEER**<br>One, and one only of these<br>in the whole wide world—<br>ROY WILLIAMS |
| **MOOSEKETEER**<br>Adults, grown-ups,<br>parents, etc. | **MOUSEKARADE**<br>HALLOWEEN Party | **MOUSEKARTOON**<br>WALT DISNEY Cartoon |
| **MOUSEKATUNE**<br>Song, any kind | **MEESKA-MOUSEKA-MOUSEKETEER**<br>Magic word better than<br>Abra-ca-dabra | **MOUSEKAMESS**<br>Rumpled, in dress, or in<br>your Mousekaroom |
| **MOUSEKATEEVEE**<br>Television at five o'clock on ABC.<br>Magic that happens only at<br>this time of day | **MOUSEKERIDDLES**<br>Riddles | **MOUSEGETAR**<br>A tenor guitar, with trade<br>mark of Mickey Mouse on it<br>(four strings) |
| **MOUSEKAMAMMA**<br>Mother synonym:<br>Mrs. Mouseketeer | **MOUSEKAPAPPA**<br>Father synonym:<br>Mr. Mouseketeer | **MOUSEKAMANCHE**<br>Indians |
| **MOUSEKAMUSIC**<br>Music at its very best | **MOUSEKEBOODLE**<br>The whole bunch of us | **MOUSEKAPLAY**<br>Fair play, playing<br>with others cheerfully |
| **MOUSEKAMIXER**<br>Used for making Mousekamalts<br>(Also) Chaperone for party | **MOUSEKADANCE**<br>Dance done by Meeseketeers,<br>Mouseketeers | **MOUSEKA MYSTERY**<br>I don't know |

*The official Mousekadictionary and member-
ship card*

WELCOME TO THE MICKEY MOUSE CLUB.
THIS OFFICIAL MEMBERSHIP CARD IS YOUR
OWN PERSONAL IDENTIFICATION.

BE SURE TO KEEP YOUR
OFFICIAL MEMBERSHIP CARD
WITH YOU AT ALL TIMES,
AND TO BE A GOOD MOUSEKETEER.

COPYRIGHT
WALT DISNEY
PRODUCTIONS

## Hi MOUSEKETEER!

OFFICIAL MEMBERSHIP CARD
**MICKEY MOUSE CLUB**

© Walt Disney Productions

NAME_____
ADDRESS_____
CITY_____ STATE_____
BIRTHDATE: MO._____ DAY_____ YR._____

NON-TRANSFERABLE

DETACH CARD AND KEEP IN
YOUR PURSE OR WALLET.

*Thursday—Pets and Hobbies*
*Friday—Surprises, Parties, and Contests.*

*These categories are not rigid however, and frequently the activity type of one night may easily be duplicated on another night. This is preferable, I believe, as a too-mechanical pattern for each night is not desirable. Each program should have a feeling of just "happening"—rather than a sense of being planned beforehand.*

Of these notes and suggestions, some found their way into the final Mickey Mouse Club product. Many did not. The emphasis on cartoons would remain, including the use of "standardized" animated segments. But the cast structure of magicians, genii, clowns, and a studio audience would be cut in favor of something more original and, in the long-run, with far greater impact.

A Disney Studio memo, dated March 23, 1955, carries a very simple line near the top of the page:

*Call kids Mouseketeers—get costumes, sweaters, little hats*

And directly under this is an equally important note:

*Audience not necessary, just kids*

The studio audience, a mainstay of much afternoon children's programming in the 1950s, from Howdy Doody to Pinky Lee, had been let go in favor of a more memorable entity: the merry Mouseketeers.

From the very beginning, Walt Disney saw the Mickey Mouse Club as a vehicle for child performers—an idea to strike terror in the heart of any producer. The whole concept of the show was unwieldy enough—five hours a week, combining animation, live-action film, original music, a large cast, guests, and special features — but five hours a week *with children* was a truly fearsome task. Disney knew from the first that he needed a couple of adults, apart from guest stars, to appear regularly on the program to lend warmth and authority. He and Bill Walsh chose from the studio's talent at hand.

**Walsh:** *We were looking for talent wherever we could find it. We were grabbing the janitor right off of his broom. I was going after everything and nothing.*

Jimmie Dodd had written a song for the "Disneyland" series which had impressed Disney enough to put the composer-lyricist-actor-singer-dancer on the permanent music staff. Disney now selected him as head Mouseketeer.

**Jimmie:** *Children just seem to take to me and I to them. Walt noticed and that's how I became the emcee and song leader for the Mouseketeers.*

Jimmie's qualifications were actually twofold. Professionally, he had worked in dozens of films, had played the guitar, and had made a television debut with Arthur Godfrey. And in his private life he was devoutly religious, perfectly in tune with the Disney brand of family entertainment.

**Jimmie:** *People have been a big factor in my career, of course, but the Lord has done it all. Help has come to me through the people the Lord has used.*

Roy Williams, a sketch artist for Walt Disney, reveals Dodd's personality in this anecdote.

**Roy:** *When Jimmie would come over here to the house, he'd bring his guitar and sing songs . . . some he'd just written for the MMC . . . he wrote the most wonderful songs in the world for the show. He was an unusually fine Christian man. He was president of the Hollywood Christian Group which Roy Rogers and Dale Evans belonged to. One night we had the whole group over here with Roy Rogers and Dale Evans; we rented chairs from Abbey Rents, and we had a nice party there in the back. We all sang hymns and talked . . . had a good get-together. Jimmie loved God so much and God created children and everything else. He was a wonderful man. One of the nicest people I've known in my life was Jimmie Dodd.*

His spiritual qualifications for the post of head Mouseketeer seem to have matched his professional capabilities. Jimmie had a positive outlook, a Christian lifestyle, and a wholesome appearance that appealed to Walt Disney. The very definition of boyish, with a shock of red hair, Jimmie looked considerably younger than his forty-five years. He was an inspired choice to lead a group of smiling, scrubbed, singing, dancing youngsters.

Disney was now ready to choose a second adult Mouseketeer from his studio's fount of ready resources.

**Roy:** *We were working on the kid show, and Bill Walsh at the time was assigned as the producer to do the original format of it. Walt liked it, he sent the original ideas to me for gags, and I did them. I specialized in gags and special material to spice it up. Bill Walsh wrote what we called the clothesline, that's the story line and the format, and a gag man like me, I come in and hang the clothes on this clothesline, which are the gags. Now I might hang up a hundred of them and Bill Walsh and Walt would come in and maybe only pick five clothes on that line, ones they thought were best. And the rest they'd put away and use for future pictures. Then one day Walt looked up and said, "Say, you're fat and funny lookin', I'm gonna put you on this and call you the Big Mooseketeer." And I said, "What?" I couldn't believe it. I was no actor. I was doing gags as I had always done. I'm a gag man.*

But an actor Roy Williams became—and a singer—and a dancer—and a sort of casting director as well, for both Jimmie and Roy worked directly with Walsh and Disney at the most crucial task the project had yet to face: the selection of the Mouseketeers.

Walt Disney (left ) and Roy Williams.
Disney put Roy through art school,
and later made him the Big
Mooseketeer.

**Walsh:** *"Where are we going to get the kids," I asked Walt, "just call up the schools and see what's loose?"*

*"Wait a minute, hold it," he said. "I don't want any of those professional schools. I don't want those kids that tap dance or blow trumpets while they're tap dancing or skip rope or have curly hair like Shirley Temple or nutty mothers and things like that. I just want ordinary kids."*

*"But Walt, what if they can't do anything?"*

*"Oh, we'll teach them. Go to a school and watch the kids at recess. Watch what happens to you. You'll notice that you're watching one kid. Not any of the other kids, but sooner or later your gaze will always go back to this one kid. That kid has star quality. Not a lot of star quality, maybe, but there's always a reason why you're watching that one kid. That's the kid we want to get in the Mouse Club."*

*Well, I wound up going to places like Alhambra, watching kids at play. I don't know what people thought, but I watched kids at play.*

From playgrounds, schoolyards, and local talent contests, children were finally brought to the studio to audition. Dodd, Williams, and Walsh worked together at making a selection, with Walt Disney himself giving most of the applicants a careful personal screening for personality, poise, appearance, and musical ability.

Of the hundreds of juvenile hopefuls, only twenty-four were picked. Many of them happened to have taken dancing lessons or singing lessons at an earlier age, but only a few were professional children with a genuine career interest beyond the moment. Very few of their parents were in show business. They were a clever group of kids who sang, danced, and played games with genuine enthusiasm. Darlene Gillespie, one of these originial Mouseketeers, recounted her MMC audition on an NBC "Tomorrow" show, in January, 1975.

**Darlene:** *I went down there, very honestly, by accident. I went down with a group of other girls because I wanted to see what his studio looked like. And, you know, I did a little dance number because I had taken dancing lessons with these four other girls and then they said to us, 'cause I guess they were looking for rounded talents, they said, "Can any of you sing?" And I really was very innocent about it and I said, "Sure." And I sang. I honest to God didn't do it like someone would say, "What a sharp kid. She sang 'Davy Crockett,' the favorite number. I sang it, honestly, because I really liked it. And, I guess, they liked it too. And that was it.*

**Roy:** *I had a big easel which I used, and I would roughly sketch the different acts with their names underneath so we would remember what they had done—ballet, dancing, or singing. They were sort of shorthand drawings to remember the different children with, besides the photographs we took. I'll never forget when Annette came out. She was a ballerina and she was spinning around. She was a beautiful girl. I said, "Oh, let's get that girl. She is out of this world." Bill Walsh and Jimmie, everybody thought she was outstanding.*

30

*Roy and Jimmie in April, 1955, with storyboards for two early Fun with Music segments: "Old MacDonald" (top) and "The Shoe Song" (bottom).*

# We Are the Merry Mouseketeers!

Out of hundreds of children who auditioned, twenty-four were chosen to inaugurate the club's first season. Here they are and here's how some of them looked in studio snapshots taken at the tryout.

## Nancy Abbate
Nancy was born on June 19, 1942, in Los Angeles, and became a Mouseketeer at twelve after a singing, dancing, and piano-playing background.

## Sharon Baird
Sharon was born in Seattle, Washington, on August 16, 1943. She first appeared in the Twentieth Century-Fox motion picture, *Bloodhounds of Broadway* as a song-and-dance child with Mitzi Gaynor. She performed regularly with Donald O'Connor, and for two years was under contract to Eddie Cantor for frequent appearances on the "Colgate Comedy Hour."

## Billie Jean Beanblossom
Billie Jean was born on New Year's Day, 1944, in Fort Worth, Texas. She had been dancing since she was four and joined the Mouseketeer regulars at eleven.

## Bobby Burgess
Bobby was born on May 19, 1941, in Long Beach, California, and dancing was his first and constant love. He auditioned originally for "Spin and Marty" but didn't make it. When called back, he did a barefoot jazz dance to "Rock Around the Clock" and was signed at the age of fourteen. He was expert at ballroom, tap, and Hawaiian dancing.

## Lonnie Burr
Lonnie was born in Dayton, Kentucky, on May 31, 1943. A professional dancer and singer at five, Lonnie became an original Mouseketeer at twelve.

## Tommy Cole
Tommy was born in Burbank, California, on December 20, 1941. At age thirteen, he auditioned for the club as an accordionist, but it was his singing that gained the attention of the Disney casting office. Tommy's appearance with the Mouseketeers was his first professional work, and soon thereafter he teamed with Darlene Gillespie to record "I Am Not Now and Never Have Been in Love."

**Nancy Abbate**

**Billie Jean Beanblossom**

**Sharon Baird**

**Lonnie Burr**

**Tommy Cole**

**Bobby Burgess**

### Dennis Day

Dennis was born on July 12, 1942, in Las Vegas, Nevada. He appeared in pictures when he was six and became a Mouseketeer when he was thirteen.

### Mary Espinosa

Mary was born January 16, 1945, in Los Angeles, and became a Mouseketeer as a ten-year-old dancer.

### Annette Funicello

Annette was born in Utica, New York, on October 22, 1942. She had started taking ballet lessons at four. Walt Disney saw her dance one summer evening at Burbank's Starlite Bowl, in a youthful "Swan Lake." She was twelve when her part-time dancing and modeling career took a sudden turn and Disney signed her with an exclusive contract.

### Darlene Gillespie

Darlene was born on April 8, 1941, in Montreal, Canada. Her mother and father, a retired song-and-dance team, sent her to dancing school at an early age. Walt Disney spotted freckle-faced Darlene when she was fourteen.

### Bonni Lou Kern

Bonni was born in Los Angeles on January 2, 1941. She specialized in acrobatics and character dancing from other countries.

### Carl "Cubby" O'Brien

Cubby was born in Burbank, California, on July 14, 1946, and first appeared on TV on the "Ray Bolger Show." Walt Disney saw the show, which featured the young drummer pounding out a beat on ashcans and cola boxes.

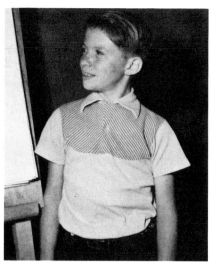

Dennis Day

Annette Funicello

Mary Espinosa

Bonni Lou Kern

Carl "Cubby" O'Brien

Darlene Gillespie

### Karen Pendleton

Karen was born in Glendale, California, on July 1, 1946. She stood 4 feet, 3½ inches tall and weighed sixty-four pounds when Disney teamed her with Cubby O'Brien as Meesketeers.

### Mary Sartori

Mary was born in Glendale, California, on January 4, 1943. A Mouseketeer at twelve, she was an accomplished dancer.

### Bronson Scott

Bronson was born in San Gabriel, California, on July 21, 1947, making her the youngest Mouseketeer. She played the piano and specialized in all types of dancing.

### Michael Smith

Michael was born on August 29, 1945, in Burbank, California. His special talents were singing, tap dancing, and square dancing.

### Mark Sutherland

Mark was born in Orange, California, December 17, 1944. He had worked with his two brothers in dance acts, on television, and in motion pictures before becoming a Mouseketeer at ten.

### Don Underhill

Don was born on September 5, 1941, in Alhambra, California. He was a talented dancer who joined the other first-year Mouseketeers.

Karen Pendleton

Bronson Scott

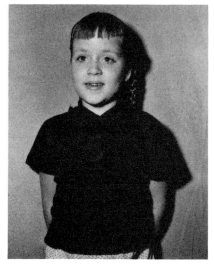

Mary Sartori

Mark Sutherland

Michael Smith

Don Underhill

### Johnny Crawford

Johnny was born in Los Angeles, on March 26, 1946. He was an ardent fencing enthusiast, with ambitions to become an actor, singer, and dancer.

### Dickie Dodd

Dickie was born in Hermosa Beach, California, on October 27, 1945. He auditioned for the club as an accordion player.

### Judy Harriet

Judy was born September 13, 1942, in Los Angeles. A classical pianist, singer, and actress, she had already spent eight years as a professional entertainer before joining the club under a seven-year contract with Walt Disney Productions.

### John Lee Johann

John was born in Madison, Wisconsin, on December 23, 1942, and became a Mouseketeer at twelve.

### Ronnie Steiner

Ronnie was born on November 21, 1942, in Winnipeg, Canada. He loved dancing and music.

### Doreen Tracey

Doreen was born April 3, 1943, in London, England, and came from a theatrical family. A dancing specialist, Doreen joined the club when she was twelve.

**Doreen Tracey**

Johnny Crawford

**Dickie Dodd**

John Lee Johann

**Ronnie Steiner**

Judy Harriet

In addition to these twenty-four, there were three original Mouseketeers who did not remain in the club for more than a few shows.

## Paul Peterson

Paul was born in Glendale, California, on September 23, 1945, and was selected for the club at the age of nine. He had some problems adjusting to the demands made of him at that early age, and his contract was dropped after the first season. He subsequently became something of a TV idol at twelve, when he joined the regular cast of "The Donna Reed Show."

## Tim and Mickey Rooney, Jr.

Tim and Mickey (unpictured) were the two original Mouseketeers with illustrious parentage. Sons of former child star Mickey Rooney, they, too, were with the club only a very short time. Cubby O'Brien remembered this about them on the "Tomorrow" show:

*One day, they went to the painters' shop where there were gallons of paint, and they mixed it all together—the black in with the brown and the brown in with the yellow. It didn't go over too big with the painters. They weren't around too long after that.*

For the Mickey Mouse Club's second season on the air, only Sharon, Bobby, Tommy, Lonnie, Dennis, Annette, Darlene, Cubby, Karen, and Doreen returned. To round things out, seven new Mouseketeers were added:

## Sherry Allen

Sherry was born December 2, 1946, and began dancing lessons at age two-and-one-half. She had made frequent public appearances years before becoming a Mouseketeer at ten.

## Eileen Diamond

Eileen was born June 15, 1943, and first appeared on TV as a model for children's clothes. Later, she danced with a ballet company in Hollywood and on television with Eleanor Powell.

## Cheryl Holdridge

Cheryl was born June 20, 1944. An actress and dancer before joining the club, she appeared in the film version of *Carousel*.

## Charley Laney

Charley was born June 18, 1943. He began taking dancing lessons at three and won his first dance contest at five.

## Larry Larsen

Larry was born September 3, 1939, making him one of the oldest Mouseketeers. He specialized in tap dancing and modern jazz dancing.

**Larry Larsen**

Paul Peterson

**Sherry Allen**

Cheryl Holdridge

Eileen Diamond

**Charley Laney**

### Jay-Jay Solari

Jay-Jay was born September 12, 1943, and was a tap dancer in motion pictures, on television, and stage.

### Margene Storey

Margene was born July 21, 1943. She auditioned for the Mickey Mouse Club as a dancer.

Of the seven newcomers, only Cheryl remained for the third season. Two-year veterans Sharon, Bobby, Lonnie, Tommy, Annette, Darlene, Cubby, Karen, and Doreen returned as well. These ten were joined by four additions:

### Don Agrati (Don Grady)

Don was born in San Diego, California, on June 8, 1944. An accomplished dancer, musician, and master of nine instruments, Don won an audition at San Francisco's Cow Palace and was signed as a Mouseketeer at thirteen.

### Bonnie Lynn Fields

Bonnie was born July 18, 1944, in Waterboro, South Carolina, and made her professional debut in the ballet presentation of the *Nutcracker Suite* at the Greek Theater in Los Angeles.

### Linda Hughes

Linda was born October 22, 1946, in San Diego, California. She was a singer, dancer, and skillful baton twirler.

### Lynn Ready

Lynn was born in Dallas, Texas, on December 3, 1944. He made his debut as an entertainer at the age of three on television and radio shows in Texas. Lynn played the steel guitar and piano.

Jay-Jay Solari

Lynn Ready

Margene Storey

Linda Hughes

Bonnie Lynn Fields

Don Agrati (Don Grady)

# Jimmie Dodd

Born in Cincinnati in 1910, Jimmie studied acting with Patia Power, and worked up a professional dance act with her teenaged son Tyrone. Moving to St. Petersburg, Florida, he played guitar and sang for a dollar a program on radio station WSUN. He tried Nashville next, and finally settled in California, where he toured the Golden State's nightclub circuit, made apearances with band leader Louis Prima, and in 1939, broke into pictures with the film *Those Were the Days,* starring William Holden.

A heart condition kept Jimmie out of the armed forces during World War II, but he and his wife, Ruth Carroll, a former dancer, joined the USO to entertain servicemen throughout Asia and North Africa. While on an overseas stint, Jimmie met Jinx Falkenburg, who got him started in television, first with Arthur Godfrey, and then on Jinx's own show.

For the Mickey Mouse Club, he acted, sang, played music, and composed over thirty-two songs, including "The Mickey Mouse March," "The Merry Mouseketeers," "Today is Tuesday," "Here Comes the Circus," "Anything Can Happen Day," "Pussy Cat Polka," and "Do What the Good Book Says," which he wrote with his wife.

# Roy Williams

Roy Williams, a cartoonist turned actor-comic, was born on July 30, 1907, in Colville, Washington, but came to Los Angeles as a child. He majored in art at Fremont High School, and was hired by Walt Disney at age eighteen. For the next three years, Disney paid for Roy's training at Los Angeles' Chouinard Art School.

Roy first worked as an artist on the Mickey Mouse cartoon strips and later moved into the story department. He received story credit on *Saludos Amigos, The Three Caballeros,* and *Make Mine Music.* His influence on the other Disney artists has been widespread and acknowledged. Outside the Disney studio, Roy's cartoons have been published in such magazines as *The New Yorker, Collier's, Liberty, This Week,* and *True.* E. P. Dutton and Company published a collection of his non-Disney cartoons under the title *How's the Back View Coming?*

# Rehearsals and Beyond

A beginning Mouseketeer was paid $185 a week, which increased with each yearly contract. Twenty percent of the total amount was invested by the studio in United States Savings Bonds and kept in trust until the children reached their twenty-first birthdays. Educational needs or an early marriage could, however, prompt release of the money as early as age eighteen.

Although California state law also required that each child have a guardian on the set at all times, overly ambitious stage mothers were something that Disney did not tolerate. When the kids were performing before the cameras, parents were banned from the sound stage. They brought their children to the studio and spent the rest of the day in an adjacent lounge area playing cards, knitting, or chatting.

**Walsh:** *Even the parents were good. My life could have been impossible with all those mothers, but they were sort of roped off in one area and they didn't bother me at all. I have an especially happy memory of Mrs. Funicello. She always used to make me a cheese cake — an Italian cheesecake—for Christmas. With ricotta. It was not all bad, believe me.*

California state law further required that each child performer spend a minimum of four hours a day in school. Two large auto-trailer schoolhouses were accordingly constructed and these air-conditioned, Disney mobile classrooms followed the Mouseketeers out on location when shooting schedules demanded. The instructor, Mrs. Jean Seaman, taught over forty subjects, including all types of elementary math, English, French, and Spanish, in a curriculum individually tailored to a class whose ages ranged from eight to fourteen. Approximately half the Mouseketeers went to school in the trailer while the other half rehearsed or filmed club segments. Then in the afternoon, the groups changed places. During summer vacation, the troupe performed for a full eight hours a day.

Sidney Miller and Dik Darley were the directors who worked most personally with the Mouseketeers. Miller staged the Fun with Music, Guest Star Day and Talent Roundup segments, planning and rehearsing the dance numbers in a manner that made the children feel that they were playing a game. Perhaps he was adept at working with children because he had been a child star himself. His playmates and co-workers in the 1930s included Jackie Cooper, Judy Garland, Mickey Rooney, and Shirley Temple.

In all, nearly 200 directors, general coordinators, production supervisors, writers, composers, musicians, artists, technicians, designers, and cameramen were responsible for the Mickey Mouse Club. The services of fifteen cameramen, twenty-three film editors, fourteen composers, two

*The Mouseketeers in the schoolhouse trailer on the Disney lot (1956).*

*Lunch in the commissary.*

46

choreographers, six set directors, and four makeup artists were required. A large staff, headed by Bob Jackman, turned out a staggering amount of music—about a song a day for three years. Chuck Keehne, in charge of costuming, worked with a tailor, dressmaker, and a wardrobe staff of six to coordinate Mouseketeer outfits, western suits, and a continuing array of special costumes. The effort was both demanding and expensive. Production costs exceeded $14,000,000 by the end of the four-year run.

Walt Disney himself worked with the show constantly, revising segments and reserving the final word on policy and good taste. Bill Walsh, as overall producer, was assisted by a large group of associate producers, production managers, and supervisors, with Hal Adelquist, Chuck Dargan, Lou Debney, Mike Holoboff, and Tommy Walker among his most active associates.

Studio veteran Hal Adelquist had been Walt's first traffic boy, and since 1954 had been director-producer on the "Disneyland" TV show. He performed the same function on many of the Mouseketeer segments. Lou Debney specialized in musical routines.

**Walsh:** *It was hysteria. It was like a Chinese firedrill. But it was fun because we'd have meetings in the morning with the kids, then we'd meet with the writers, then with the guy who did the sets and the costumes. After lunch everyone would meet again. By that time, we all would contribute ideas about props, sets, wardrobe, music, and about three o'clock that afternoon we'd shoot it. It was fresh; you didn't have time to get over-rehearsed.*

And how did this working arrangement affect the mousekids? On the NBC "Tomorrow" show (January, 1975), several of them looked back and described to host Tom Snyder, how it felt to be a Mouseketeer.

**Tom Snyder:** *Did you all have little, petty fights or jealousies? I mean you were kids then, and I bet you were allowed to have those things . . .*

**Lonnie:** *Defensive stuff. . . .What we called "chopping" then.*

**Tom Snyder:** *What would you fight over?*

**Lonnie:** *Oh, somebody would say something. Like once I said to one of the girls—we were chopping back and forth—and I said something which sounds silly now. "You're not old enough to shave your legs yet." That was a big insult. And then we wouldn't talk for two days.*

**Tom Snyder:** *But it never happened that the director would have to come out and say, "All right kids, now just cut this out."*

**Tommy:** *No, I think we were all pretty professional on that end of it.*

**Lonnie:** *One time Tommy and I had a fight.*

Production reports like this one keep track of time use and expenses. Everything from the cast's working hours to the amount of coffee consumed gets reported. Notice that the Mouseketeers work from 8:30 A.M. to 4:45 P.M., with a one-hour break for lunch.

## WALT DISNEY PRODUCTIONS
## DAILY PRODUCTION REPORT

**Shooting Schedule and Status**

| | 1st Unit | Holi-days | Trav-el | Pre-Prod. | Post-Prod. | 2nd Unit |
|---|---|---|---|---|---|---|
| No. Days Scheduled | | | | | | |
| No. Days Revised | | | | | | |

**Number of Days on Picture Including Today**

| Rehear-sals | Lay-off | Trav-el | Holi-days | 2nd Unit | Re-takes | Shoot-ing |
|---|---|---|---|---|---|---|
| | | | | | | 2 |

Director __DIK DARLEY__
Working Title __MICKEY MOUSE TV CLUB__
Producer __WALT DISNEY__

Date __MONDAY, OCTOBER 24, 1955__
Picture No. __8233 & 8223__   Date Started __
Scheduled Finish Date __   Revised __

Set __TREASURE MINE 8233-041-046-051 - 3346-825 -- 8223-044-045-046-048__
Set No. __SEE ABOVE__   Location __STAGE #1__
Shooting Call __9:00 AM__   Crew Calls __8:00 AM__   First Shot __10:20 AM__   Last Shot __6:05 PM__
1st Meal Period __11:50 - 12:50__   2nd Meal Period __   Company Dismissed { On Location __   At Studio __6:05 PM__

FOR REMARKS AND EXPLANATION OF DELAYS SEE OTHER SIDE

| SCRIPT SCENES AND PAGES | | | MINUTES | | SETUPS | | ADDED SCENES | | STILLS | | | RETAKES | |
|---|---|---|---|---|---|---|---|---|---|---|---|---|---|
| | Scenes | Pages | | | | | | | Prod. | Publicity | | Pages | Scenes |
| | | | Prev. — | | Prev. — | | Prev. | Prev. | | | Prev. | | |
| Original Script | | | Today 14:43 | | Today 20 | | Today | Today | | | Today | | |
| Additions | | | Total 14:43 | | Total 20 | | Total | Total | | | Total | | |
| Deletions | | | | | | | | | | | | | |
| Revised Total | | | Scene No. | 8223-044 | SCS.: | 44-44A | | | | | | | |
| | | | " | 8223-045 | SCS.: | 45-45A | | | | | | | |
| Taken Prev. | | | XXXXXX | 8223-046 | SCS.: | 46-46A | | | | | | | |
| | | | " | 8223-048 | SCS.: | 48 | | | | | | | |
| Taken Today | 12 | 8 | XXXXXXXX | 8233-041 | SCS.: | 41 | | | | | | | |
| | | | " | 8233-046 | SCS.: | 46 | | | | | | | |
| Total to Date | 12 | 8 | XXXXXX | 8233-051 | SCS.: | 51 | | | | | | | |
| | | | | 3346-825 | SCS.: | 25-26P | | | | | | | |
| To Be Taken | | | Sound Tracks | | | | | | | | | | |

| PICTURE NEGATIVE | | | | | SOUND TRACK POSITIVE | | | | MEALS | |
|---|---|---|---|---|---|---|---|---|---|---|
| USED | | WASTE | PRINTED | | PRINTED | | WASTE | | | |
| Used Prev. — | Prev. — | | | | Used Prev. | Prev. | | | Breakfasts | |
| Used Today 6,020 | Today 720 | | 2,280 | | Used Today | Today | | | Lunches | |
| Used to Date 6,020 | To Date 720 | | 2,280 | | Used to Date | To Date | | | Dinners | |
| 2nd Unit — | 2nd Unit — | | — | | 2nd Unit | 2nd Unit | | | Suppers | |
| Total Used to Date 6,020 | Estimated — | | | | Total Used to Date | Estimated | | | 5 Gal. Coffee | |

| CAST — Weekly and Day Players Worked—W Rehearsal—R Finished—F Started—S Hold—H Test—T Travel—Tv | W S R T | H F T Tv | First Call | Time In | Set Call | Time on Set | Time Dismissed | Hours Out for Meals | EXTRAS USED | |
|---|---|---|---|---|---|---|---|---|---|---|
| 1 JIMMIE DODD | W | | 8:30 | 8:30 | 9:00 | 9:00 | 6:05 | 1 | No.: 1 | 1 |
| 2 | | | | | | | | | Rate: 29.00 | 29.00 |
| 3 BILLIE JEAN BEANBLOSSOM | W | | " | " | " | " | 5:30 | 1 | Call: 8:30 | 9:00 |
| 4 MARY ESPINOSA | W | | " | " | " | " | " | 1 | Finish: 5:30 | 5:45 |
| 5 BRONSON SCOTT | W | | " | " | " | " | " | 1 | Arrive: Welfare Workers | |
| 6 MARK SUTHERLAND | W | | " | " | " | " | " | 1 | No.: | |
| 7 BONNI KERN | W | | " | " | " | " | " | 1 | Rate: | |
| 8 DON UNDERHILL | W | | " | " | " | " | " | 1 | Call: | |
| 9 | | | | | | | | | Finish: | |
| 10 BOBBY BURGESS | W | | 9:00 | 9:00 | 9:00 | 9:00 | 5:45 | 1 | Arrive: | |
| 11 MARY SARTORI | W | | " | " | " | " | " | 1 | No.: | |
| 12 JUDY HARRIET | W | | " | " | " | " | " | 1 | Rate: | |
| 13 TOMMY COLE | W | | " | " | " | " | " | 1 | Call: | |
| 14 SHARON BAIRD | W | | " | " | " | " | " | 1 | Finish: | |
| 15 ANNETTE FUNICELLO | W | | " | " | " | " | " | 1 | Arrive: | |
| 16 KAREN PENDELTON | W | | " | " | " | " | " | 1 | No.: | |
| 17 CUBBY O'BRIEN | W | | " | " | " | " | " | 1 | Rate: | |
| 18 LONNIE BURR | W | | " | " | " | " | " | 1 | Call: | |
| 19 DENNIS DAY | W | | " | " | " | " | " | 1 | Finish: | |
| 20 MIKE SMITH | W | | " | " | " | " | " | 1 | Arrive: | |
| 21 DOREEN TRACY | W | | " | " | " | " | " | 1 | No.: | |
| 22 | | | | | | | | | Rate: | |
| 23 BOB AMSBERRY | W | | 1:00 | 1:00 | 1:00 | 1:00 | 5:45 | — | Call: | |
| 24 | | | | | | | | | Finish: | |
| 25 | | | | | | | | | Arrive: | |
| 26 | | | | | | | | | Total Extras: Standins: | |
| 27 | | | | | | | | | Total Adjustments: | |
| 28 | | | | | | | | | 1st Meal: | |
| 29 | | | | | | | | | 2nd Meal: | |
| 30 | | | | | | | | | Remarks: | |
| 31 | | | | | | | | | | |

__BEN CHAPMAN__
Production Manager

__
Unit Manager

TL   __JACK CUNNINGHAM—TOMMY THOMPSON__
Assistant Director

**Tommy:** *Oh, yeah. We had a little fist fight there, but it didn't last too long.*

**Lonnie:** *What happened was this. We were just hitting in the body, and Tommy hit me in the face by accident. Doreen said, "Tommy's fighting dirty, he hit Lonnie in the face." And I got mad and hit him in the ear, he fell down, and my mother broke it up.*

**Darlene:** *I think the biggest contest was between Tommy and Lonnie and Bobby, and that was pompadours. . . . I think that was a sign of virility at their age, who had the highest, tallest pompadour. It was something else, because they'd make them comb their hair down, right? And then the boys would sneak in the bathroom and rat it up and make it look bigger. It was hilarious.*

**Tommy:** *Wardrobe people would come around. They didn't want to see any hair in front. And they'd push your hat down and you'd look terrible. . . .*

**Cubby:** *I think everybody had a little bit of their own identity on that show. And they gave each one of us a chance to show what we could do. I think that's basically why it was such a good show.*

**Cheryl:** *And we were also fortunate that we were with a group of kids. We weren't just isolated, like a lot of children in show business, with only adults. We had kids around us. That kept us pretty normal.*

**Tommy:** *The Disney studio kept us normal. Because the Disney studio was a fantastic studio for kids to work. There's no swearing on the set, or very, very rarely any swear words around kids. I'm sure an adult show. . . .*

**Darlene:** *They'd go in the washroom maybe.*

**Lonnie:** *Sidney would forget every once in a while.*

**Tommy:** *Our director.*

**Lonnie:** *A very strong director.*

**Darlene:** *I think the most important thing is, I don't think any of the kids felt they were stars, or really big, important people. . . .*

**Cubby:** *I was having fun. I wouldn't want to change it for anything.*

**Cheryl:** *We were treated well.*

*Mouseketeers in rehearsal. Karen and Cubby (right) are wearing practice togs to simulate their show costumes.*

# The Club on the Air

Who's the leader of the club
That's made for you and me?
M–I–C–K–E–Y  M–O–U–S–E...
Yea, Mickey! Yea, Mickey!
Yea, Mickey Mouse Club!

## Monday

Hi, Mouseketeers! Big doings this week—adventure, fun, music, cartoons, news... Everybody ready? Then on with the show!

*On Mondays, Mickey opens the show garbed as a song-and-dance-man, because Monday is Fun with Music Day. Following the opening (and a commercial), a "Mickey Mouse Club Newsreel" is shown. It can be anything from "Kiddy Kar Klass," spotlighting a miniature highway in Phoenix, Arizona, on which grade-schoolers serve as traffic cops, to the "Festival of the Ages," celebrated in Kyoto, Japan. Photographed by camera teams around the world and narrated by children for children, a new newsreel was shown in the first quarter-hour segment of the show on Mondays, Wednesdays, and Fridays, during the club's first and second seasons on the air (1955–57).*

*After the newsreel, the Mouseketeers make their entrance to sing "Fun with Music," and introduce themselves to the audience in the Mouseketeer Roll Call and theme song ("We are the merry mouseketeers..."). Ears in place and introductions accomplished, Fun with Music Day proceeds with a full-scale Mousekemusical, like...*

*"The Pussycat Polka"...*

*..."Hi to You"...*

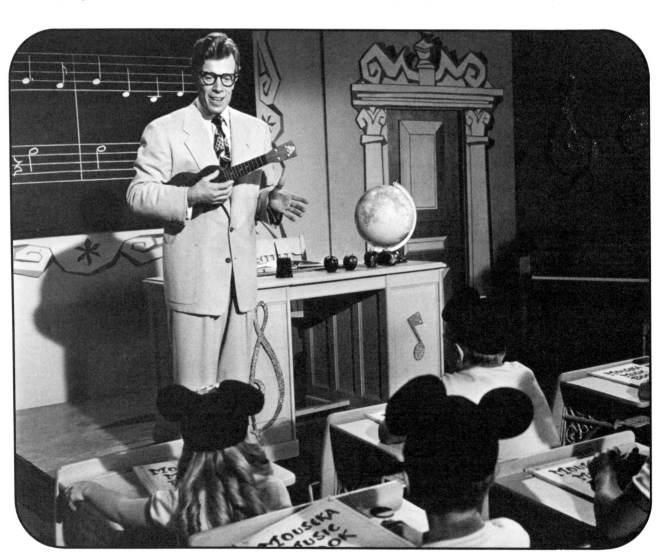

*..."Mousegetar Lesson."*

Other Mousekemusicals include "Mixed-up Mother Goose," "Hiawatha," "A Cowboy Needs a Horse," "The Tramp Ballet," "An Evening with Darlene," trips to "Paris," "Switzerland," "The Malt Shop," and...

...*"Cooking with Minnie Mouse"* (right). Besides Doreen and Bobby, pictured here, this Mousekemusical included Mrs. Ruth Dodd.

*"The Shoe Song"* (below). A number featuring shoes and their uses. Karen and Cubby, perpetually teamed, conclude the number as a bridal couple.

# Tuesday

Hi, Mouseketeers! Got guests coming and everything! Everybody neat and pretty? Then.. take it away!

*Mickey, done up as a concert pianist, is anxious to confirm his club members' neatness and prettiness because—*

Today is Tuesday
You know what that means—
We're gonna have a special guest!

*After the Guest Star song, pictured below, and Mouseketeer Roll Call, Tuesday proceeds with an adult performer (right) working with the mousekids or on his own.*

*Morey Amsterdam (comic/cellist)*

Other guest stars included Judy Canova, Donna Atwood, José Carioca, "Balloon Man" Wally Boag, the Mellowmen, and...

*Carla Alberghetti (singer)*

*Cliff "Ukelele Ike" Edwards (the voice of Jiminy Cricket)*

*Jerry Colonna (comic)*

# Wednesday

Whoa, boy! Whoa, steady!

*(The flying carpet whinnies like a horse.)*

Hi, Mouseketeers! Wednesday is Stunt Day, Mouseketeers, so hang on, anything goes. You ready? Then let the show begin!

*Wednesday is Anything Can Happen Day. After the usual Wednesday newsreel, the Mouseketeers appear in a stunning array of disguises (right) to sing:*

Today is the day
That is filled with surprises!
Nobody knows what's gonna happen!
Why, you might find yourself
On an elephant on the moon
Or riding in an auto
Underneath the blue lagoon...

*Anything can happen and just about everything does. The grab-bag of Wednesday features ranges from gymnastics exhibitions to trips to Disneyland. At right, Roy gives a drawing lesson—making an instant Mickey out of circles. Another of the Big Mooseketeer's specialties was scribble-sketching. He could make a scribble into a finished picture in six seconds flat.*

*Another "Anything" that happened (far right): a gadget band with Darlene on the Trombozoo.*

# Thursday

Hi, Mouseketeers! Well, today is . . . ah . . . oh . . . ah . . . Circus Day!

*But before the circus begins, a special guest always appears on Thursdays—Jiminy Cricket—who fills the first fifteen-minute segment with material of a patently educational nature. In his Encyclopedia series, the cricket opens with a song. (The song, incidentally, taught a generation to spell E–N–C–Y–C–L–O–P–E–D–I–A. Some of us still have trouble writing the word without recalling Jimmie Dodd's spell-binding melody.) Jiminy then presents a lecture on biology ("You—The Human Animal"), safety ("I'm No Fool"), or wildlife ("Nature of Things"). These segments combined live-action footage, animation, and music.*

Use the En–cyclopedia!
E–N–C–Y–C–L–O–P–E–D–I–A

*After Jiminy's stint,
it's time for the circus to begin...*

Cubby and Karen (left) as strongman and stronglady.

Bob Amsberry (right) as a barker. "Uncle Bob" was the third adult Mouseketeer. He called himself the show's "utility man," as he performed a variety of small roles in many of the production numbers. He was seen, at various times, as a British Grenadier, a soda jerk, and a talking corpse. Prior to his Mousekeduties, Amsberry produced and starred on children's television shows in Oregon, and worked as a radio announcer, actor, and writer.

Here comes the circus
Everyone loves the circus
And that includes
The Merry Mouseketeers.

*Mary Espinosa (above) as the fat lady.*

*As on other days, Circus Day proceeds from a production number and roll call to a special feature, geared to the day's theme.Circus acts on the Mickey Mouse Club included lion-tamer George Keller, the Allen Bears, the tumbling Marcellis, and Kamur of India (right), who defied the law of gravity with dinner plates.*

## Friday

Yeh-ee! Yeh-ee! Hi, podners! This here is our roundup day, so you all pretty nigh ready? Sure enough? Let's get on with it!

*Talent Roundup Day, every Friday, is one of the Mickey Mouse Club's most innovative segments. To put it together Hal Adelquist coordinated a national talent search. Department stores and markets across the country held local talent round-ups, in which the winners (contestants had to be between the ages of eight and fourteen) were presented with a studio-designed certificate (right) and were filmed by roving Disney camera teams. The Disney casting office then viewed the young-sters on film and selected winners, who were then flown to Hollywood and given spots on the Friday programs. A real glass-slipper story, from the people who brought you Cinderella. To start Talent Roundup Day, the production number and roll call took a western turn:*

Saddle your ponies, here we go
Down to the talent rodeo!

Gather up Susie, Jack, and Joe!
Join the talent roundup!

*Lorene and Linda Giel-fish, accordionists, with their singing brother Gary.*

*Applauding the Talent Roundup winners.*

*The Covans, a Los Angeles dancing group.*

Here's your hat
(What a hat)
Here's your ears...
Reach right out
Time is here
You're an honorary
Mouseketeer!

*With this jingle, the Mouseketeers present the winners with a scroll, gilded mouse ears, and a rodeo hat. Here they welcome concert pianist Jon Peterson to the ranks.*

# Serials

After the Mouseketeer segment, the third fifteen-minute segment of the original one-hour format is devoted to continuing adventures. Some, like What I Want to Be, Border Collie, Foreign Correspondent, and Christmas Round the World are of a documentary nature. But others are genuine stories, serialized fictional adventures produced especially for the club. Comprised of twenty-five to thirty episodes—each fifteen minutes in length—a series forms a complete narrative. Every episode is fitted with a cliffhanger ending, harking back to the days of the Saturday matinee. In the entire history of television, remarkably few live-action film series have been created exclusively for children. The Mickey Mouse Club serials are landmarks of the genre.

Darlene Gillespie, Chinook, and puppy in Corky and White Shadow, 1955 (top, left). The series starred Darlene, Buddy Ebsen, and Chinook, a 145-pound, white German Shepherd. In seventeen episodes, Corky and her dog pursue the Dude, a notorious bank robber, much to the concern of Corky's sheriff father (Ebsen). The tale gave Darlene a chance to sing several western ballads in the course of the action.

Tommy Kirk (left), Florenz Ames (center), and Tim Considine in The Hardy Boys: The Mystery of the Applegate Treasure, 1956 (bottom, left). Adapted from Franklin W. Dixon's The Tower Treasure, this series faithfully captures the essence of Dixon's classic juveniles. Tim and Tommy, as the sibling detectives, are aided by Carole Ann Campbell as Iola Morton. In 1957, the Hardy Boys returned in The Mystery of Ghost Farm.

Neil Wolfe (left) and Jonathan Bailey as Clint and Mac, 1957 (top, right). This series is about an American boy and his British buddy who, together, outwit a band of criminals.

Roberta Shore (left), Tim Considine, and Annette Funicello in Annette, 1957 (bottom, right). This serial with a teenaged slant was adapted from Janette Sebring Lowery's Margaret. Country-girl Annette comes to the big city to live with her aunt and uncle. Society bobby-soxer Roberta Shore is none too pleased with Annette's beauty, popularity, and talent. (Roberta, it seems, sings too). She accuses the shy newcomer of stealing a necklace. Tim Considine, David Stollery, Sharon Baird, Tommy Cole, Bonnie Lynn Fields, and Doreen Tracey are all brought into the story before the missing necklace is recovered. It fell inside a piano.

But of all the Mickey Mouse Club serials, perhaps the best remembered is . . .

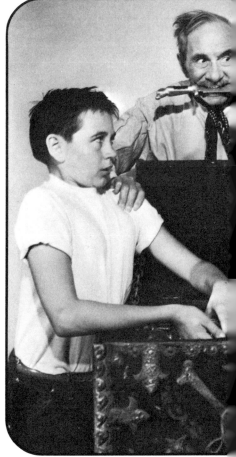

# The Adventures of Spin and Marty

*A city boy, Master Martin Markham (David Stollery) and his manservant Perkins (J. Pat O'Malley) arrive at the Triple R Ranch (a boys' camp) for a summer of "roughing it."*

*The other guys, led by Spin (Tim Considine) find Marty pretty stuck-up and spoiled. A frog-in-the-bed trick leads Spin and Marty to the boxing ring.*

*The fight ends in a draw. Marty is softening up toward the "riff-raff" and the guys are starting to like him a little better.*

*Marty conquers his fear of horses by learning to ride Skyrocket with help from counselor Bill (Harry Carey, Jr.).*

He even gets cocky enough to try to ride Skyrocket bareback, and on his own. The horse throws him.

Marty returns with his arm in a sling, and is surprised to find that the guys think it is a kind of badge. Marty is on his way.

He joins in a snipe hunt, has a joking song composed about his ride on Skyrocket, and finally gets even with Spin by joining Ambitious (B.G. Norman) in a practical joke—they dress up as ghosts.

The series ends with everyone friends—and the Triple R ready to win the local rodeo!

"Spin and Marty" was so popular, it inspired a sequel in the
1956—57 season. The boys were a little older by now, so a neighboring
girls' ranch was added to the plot, with campers Annette Funicello and
Darlene Gillespie much in evidence. Another new character,
"Moochie," was played by Kevin Corcoran. A third story, "The New
Adventures of Spin and Marty," aired in the club's third season.

# Mousekartoon Time

*The Mouseketeers have a magic chant to introduce this final segment:*

Time to Twist the Mousekedial to the Right and the Left with a Great Big Smile

This Is the Way We Get to See

A Mousekartoon for You and Me!

Meeseka Mooseka Mouseketeer
Mousekartoon Time Now Is Here

Steamboat Willie (1928)

The Old Army Game (1943)

The Ugly Duckling (1939)

Rescue Dog (1947)

Bellboy Donald (1942)

Plutopia (1951)

# *Yea, Mickey!*

According to the Nielsen Television Index report of February 1, 1956, and the Audience Research Bureau report of February, 1956, the Mickey Mouse Club reached more total viewers than any other daytime program. It reached more adults than all but eight of the twenty-five daytime programs on the air. And it reached more *children* than any other program — day or night — except "Disneyland." It held a 218% advantage in viewership over "Pinky Lee" and 135% advantage over "Howdy Doody." It was seen four to five times a week by 42% of its weekly audience. By comparison, only 14.3% of the "Pinky Lee Show's" audience tuned in with such regularity. In other words, Mickey's fans were three times as loyal. In its first Nielsen race, the club was second only to the World Series.

The key to it all was undoubtedly the Mouseketeers themselves. *Motion Picture Daily* put it well: *The Mouseketeers . . . have the lack of self-consciousness born of the knowledge that before their audience they are equals.*

Children performing for children; that's what the club was all about. The total fan mail from 1955–58 reached nearly 360,000 letters — about 7,500 a month. A number of these could be counted on to inquire whether or not a favorite Mouseketeer had been in a bus accident or had choked to death on a wad of gum. Death and injury rumors were rampant. The studio finally printed a standard postcard in answer, assuring the fans that Annette and her friends were all alive and well.

Annette's fan mail alone numbered 6,000 a month at her peak of popularity. Although she hadn't been considered any more special than the other Mouseketeers when she was hired, from the show's first week on the air the letters began to pour in. The studio began to think of her as the major source of the club's popularity. Disney himself came to regard her as a sort of yardstick. When Annette grew too old for her ears (and her sweaters) the Mickey Mouse Club was finished.

From 1962–65, the Mickey Mouse Club had a second life — in national syndication. It reached an estimated twelve million children daily in its first syndicated year. These were not new shows, but half-hour versions of the 1955–59 club. Although affiliated with no network and shown at different times in different cities by selected stations, the show was popular once again.

In 1975, a third life began — a second syndicated run. Its success prompted the writing of this book.

417
MOUSEKETEER GIRL

416
MOUSEKETEER BOY

*Ben Cooper Incorporated's three-piece Mouseketeer playsuits*

benay-Albee

SUGGESTED RETAIL
69¢

FELT #800
MIRACLE FIBER #801

#800

WALT DISNEY'S OFFICIAL

# mickey mouse hat

Cash in on this fast-selling Mickey Mouse beanie!
25,000,000 kids see it worn daily on Disney's Mouseketeer
T.V. program, coast-to-coast. It's by far the fastest selling
novelty hat today! *550,000 shipped since October!*

Now! Three models (as pictured): Mickey Mouse, Minnie
Mouse Beanies (69¢ retailers); and Mickey Mouse Turn-A-
Bout Hat: a face in the back, beanie from the front. It has
movable eyes! (98¢ retailer).

FELT #802
MIRACLE FIBER #803

ONE SIZE FITS ALL HEAD SIZES
AVAILABLE IN REPROCESSED FELT OR STRAW MIRACLE FIBER
FOR SPRING AND SUMMER WEAR!

TURN-A-BOUT HAT
#888
FELT ONLY

*Order now!*

Use this coupon.
Make your store
Mouseketeer Club Headquarters!

benay-Albee
NOVELTY COMPANY
52-01 FLUSHING AVE.
MASPETH, N. Y.

Postage
Will be Paid
by
Addressee

No
Postage Stamp
Necessary
If Mailed in the
United States

BUSINESS REPLY CARD
First Class Permit No. 22366, Sec. 34.9, P.L.&R., New York, N. Y.

BENAY-ALBEE NOVELTY CO.

52-01 Flushing Avenue

Maspeth, New York

*Mouse Hats from the Benay-Albee Novelty Co., Inc. (1956)*

*Cookies from the Kroger Company (circa 1956)*

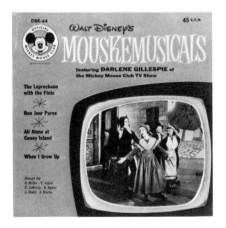

*The Mouseketeers—exclusively on Disneyland Records*

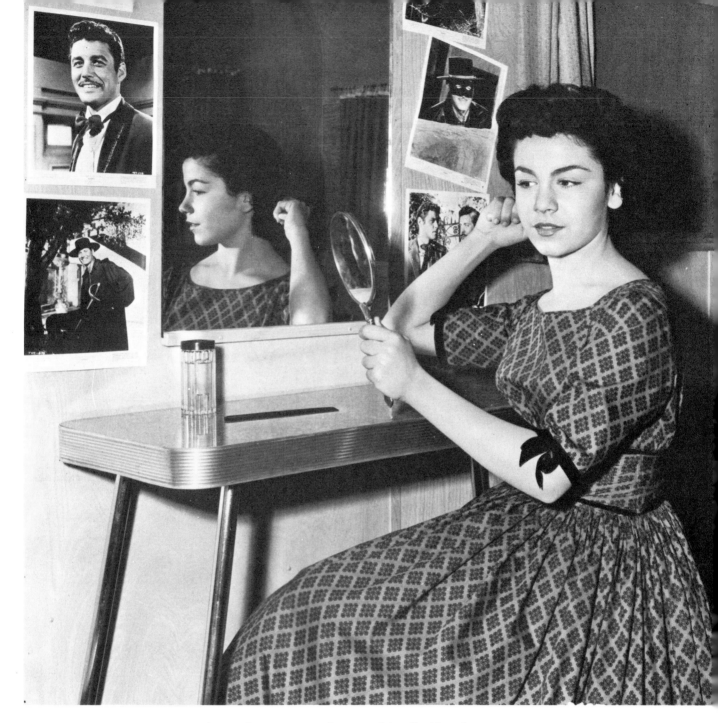

Annette became a recording star while still a Mouseketeer. "Tall Paul," "How Will I Know My Love?" and "O Dio Mio" each sold upward of 250,000 copies on Disney's Vista label. Her albums included "Annette," "Annette Sings Anka," "Hawaiianette," and "Dance Annette." When the club went off the air, the studio kept her under nonexclusive contract to star in The Shaggy Dog, and The Horsemasters. For American International, she starred in the Beach Party movies. But always associated in the public mind with Walt Disney, Annette never appeared in a truly revealing bathing suit.

Who's
the
little
lady
that
we
never
will
forget?

Annette

Annette

Annette

# Mickey Mouse Club Songbook

# Mickey Mouse Theme Song ("Minnie's Yoo Hoo")

I'm the guy they call lit-tle Mick-ey Mouse, Got a
Oh, the blue bird down in the cher-ry tree, And the

sweet-ie down in the chick-en house. Nei-ther fat nor skin-ny, she's the horse-'s whin-ny, she's my
bus-y buzz of the bum-ble bee, Eve-ning bells a ring-in', whip-poor-wills a sing-in', well they

lit-tle Min-nie Mouse. When it's feed-ing time for the an-i-mals, I just
don't mean much to me, For my heart is down in the chick-en house And I'll

howl and growl like the can-ni-bals, I just turn my heel, to the hen house steal and you
long to be with my Min-nie Mouse And I'll meet her there, mid that fra-grance rare, sing to

hear me sing this song. Oh the old tom cat with his meow, meow, meow, Old houn' dog with his
her this mel-o-dy.

Chorus:
bow, bow, bow, the crow's caw caw and the mule's hee haw Gosh what a rack-et like an old buzz saw I have

lis-tened to the cuck-oo cock his cuck-oo. And I've heard the roost-er cock his doo-dle-do-oo With the

cows and the chickens they all sound like the dick-ens when I hear my lit-tle Minnie's yoo hoo. Oh the yoo hoo.

91

# Mickey Mouse March

By
JIMMIE DODD

(Guitar or other accompaniment)

1. Mick - ey Mouse Club! Mick - ey Mouse Club!
2. We have fun and we play safe - ly!
3. Look both ways when you cross cross - ings!
4. Don't take chanc - es, play with safe - ty!
5. When you ride your bike, be care - ful!

Who's the lead - er of the club That's made for you and me?

M - I - C - K - E - Y M - O - U - S - E! Hey!

Who is march - ing coast to coast And far a - cross the sea?

# The Merry Mouseketeers

By
JIMMIE DODD

As we con - tin - ue through the years, (Through the years,)_____

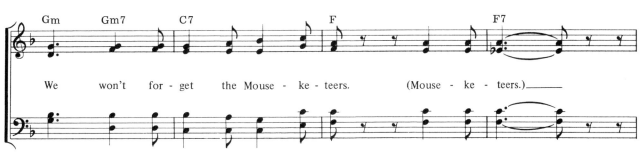

We won't for - get the Mouse - ke - teers. (Mouse - ke - teers.)_____

Hep! Two! Three! Four! Hoo - ray! Hoo - ray! Hoo - ray!_____

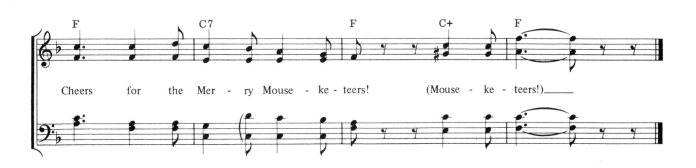

Cheers for the Mer - ry Mouse - ke - teers! (Mouse - ke - teers!)_____

# Fun with Music

Words and Music by
SID MILLER and
TOM ADAIR

# Today Is Tuesday

By
**JIMMIE DODD**

like good Mouse - ke - teers!____
We're gon - na pre - sent____ a
We're proud to pre - sent____ to

guest to - day,
you to - day,

'Cause Tues - day is "Guest star day!"_____

# Anything Can Happen Day

By
JIMMIE DODD

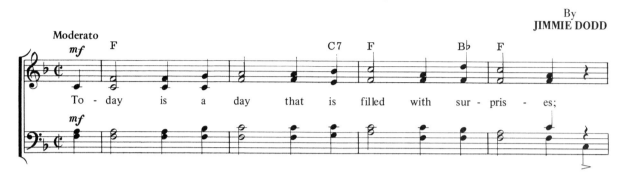

To-day is a day that is filled with sur-pris-es;

No-bod-y knows what's gon-na hap-pen!_____ Why,
(Hap-pen!)

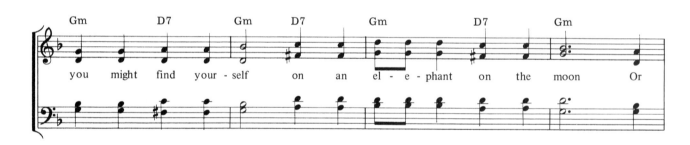

you might find your-self on an el-e-phant on the moon Or

rid-ing in an au-to un-der-neath a blue la-goon!_____ Yes,

we Mouse - ke - teers think you're gon - na have some thrills And

you know it's true that a laugh can cure your ills. And so, if

you're pleas - ure bent, We are glad to pre - sent_____ The

Mouse - ke - teers "An - y - thing Can Hap - pen Day."_____

# Here Comes the Circus!

By
JIMMIE DODD

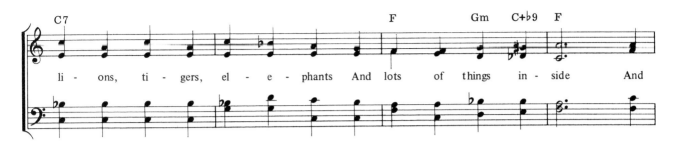

li - ons, ti - gers, el - e - phants And lots of things in - side And

there's a man who's nine feet tall And a la - dy five feet wide. And so, Hoo -

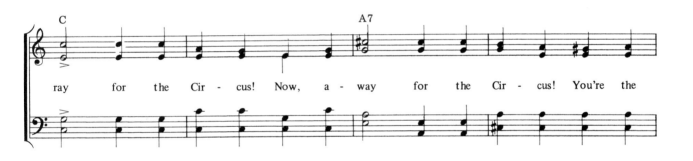

ray for the Cir - cus! Now, a - way for the Cir - cus! You're the

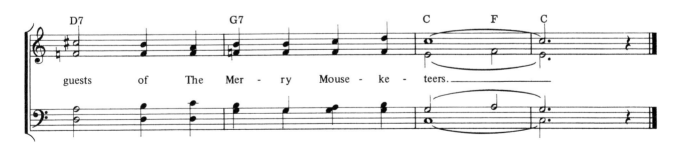

guests of The Mer - ry Mouse - ke - teers. _____

# Talent Roundup

Words by
**GIL GEORGE**

Music by
**GEORGE BRUNS**

Saddle your pony, here we go Down to the talent rodeo.

Gather up Susie, Jack and Joe, Join the talent round-up.

Round 'em up! Bring 'em in! Ev-'ry-body's sure to win!

Step right up! Here we go! Oh, what a rodeo!

Bring along Dinah, Bob and Bill, Ask ev-'ry-body on the hill,

We're gonna have a great big thrill. Join the talent round-up.

# The Triple "R" Song

Words and Music by
STAN JONES

Moderato, Not Too Slowly, And Gaily

1. Way out there on the Tri - ple "R" Yip - pi - a, Yip - pi - o The hor - ses are the best by far
2. Spin is a cow - boy, yes sir - ee Yip - pi - a, Yip - pi - o The best ev - er seen by you or me
3. Ol - lie's a wran - gler for the Tri - ple "R" Yip - pi - a, Yip - pi - o But he should a' done his ri - ding in a good used car
4. Bur - nett tells us right from wrong Yip - pi - a, Yip - pi - o And he sings a dog - gone pret - ty song
5. In the sun we're ri - ding, sing - ing Yip - pi - a, Yip - pi - o Back the ech - oes come a ring - ing

Yip - pi - a,_____ Yip - pi - o So sad - dle up, boys, and
Yip - pi - a,_____ Yip - pi - o When he jumps in the sad - dle what a
Yip - pi - a,_____ Yip - pi - o With a whoop and a hol - ler and
Yip - pi - a,_____ Yip - pi - o Once a bull chased Bur - nett
Yip - pi - a,_____ Yip - pi - o So sway in the sad - dle and

sad - dle up well, And lis - ten to the sto - ry that I have to tell.
sight to see 'Cause he's got the po - ny's tail where his head should be.
wind in his shirt Then a pitch and a thud and Ol - lie ate the dirt. Yip - pi -
through the hay But it did - n't stop his sing - ing "They went that - a way."
swing a - long And sing an - oth - er cho - rus of the Tri - ple "R" song.

*For Repeat*

a, Yip - pi - i,_____ Yip - pi - o._____

*Fine*

a,_____ Yip - pi -

*mf*  *mp*  *cresc.*  *poco  a*

i, Yip - pi - o.

*poco*  *f*  *sfz  sfz*

107

# I'm No Fool

By
**JIMMIE DODD**

**Verse:**

1. An - y - one can be a fool And do things which are wrong, But
2. An - y fool ne - glects his bike And thinks he's be - ing smart. He
3. An - y fool will load his bike So much that he can't see. He
4. Show - off is a stu - pid thing, As an - y fool should know. He
5. An - y fool gives sig - nals wrong, Or may - be not at all. He

fools find out when it's too late That they don't live so long. Oh!
does - n't give it an - y care And soon it falls a - part. Oh!
rides on side - walks, so, what hap - pens? A ca - tas - tro - phe. Oh!
thinks it's fun, but what a sor - ry End - ing to his show. Oh!
does - n't look a - head And so he's head - ing for a fall. Oh!

**Chorus:**

I'm no fool, no, sir - ee! I wan - na live to be nine - ty - three.

I play safe for you and me, 'Cause I'm no fool.

# Mousekartoon Time

By
**JIMMIE DODD**

Time to twist our mouse-ka-dial To the right and the left with a great big smile.

This is the way we get to see A Mouse-kar-toon for you and me.

Mee - ska! Mouse-ka! Mouse-ke-teer! Mouse-kar-toon time now is here!

# The Mouseketeers Today

At the close of every Mickey Mouse Club broadcast, the Mouseketeers gathered to sing, "Through the years we'll all be friends, wherever we may be." Although few of the mousekids have kept the kind of close personal contact that the song implies, most are ready for a reunion when the opportunity arises. (The opportunity does arise, incidentally, mostly on Disney Studio occasions — a big birthday for Mickey, for instance, or the launching of a new run in syndication.)

The later lives of the child performers contrast strikingly. Alumni include a wallpaper hanger, a cocktail waitress, an auto salesperson, and two secretaries. Most of them are married; five are divorced. Their present ages range from late twenties to mid-thirties. Altogether the Mouseketeers have produced about thirty children. In general, the Mouseketeers today fall into two categories: those who remained in show business and those who did not. Let these brief biographies speak for themselves:

### Johnny Crawford

Johnny went from one year as a Mouseketeer to five years (1958–63) as Chuck Connors' son on "The Rifleman." He had several Top Ten recordings in the early 1960s, made numerous guest appearances on television, and most recently starred in a Canadian-made film, *Inbreaker,* to be released this year. Johnny is a bachelor.

### Dennis Day

Dennis has directed musicals, written a dance manual, appeared in commercials, and taught dance and drama at Immaculate Heart College. Several of his works as an artist and sculptor have made their way into private collections.

### Linda Hughes

Linda is married to Myron Vaughan, a teacher. They have two children. The Vaughans reside in Los Angeles.

### Michael Smith

Michael graduated from the club to Las Vegas, "The FBI Story," and several television specials during the ten years he stayed in show business. He is now employed as a wallpaper hanger in Hollywood. Mike is single.

### Jay-Jay Solari

Jay-Jay works as a tap dance specialist, a writer, and a professional dance instructor.

### Tim Considine

Son of film producer John Considine, Jr. (*Boystown* and *Young Tom Edison*), Tim went from the Mickey Mouse Club serials to other Disney projects, including *Swamp Fox* and *The Shaggy Dog.* He was a regular on "My Three Sons," and during his run with the series began writing for the show with his brother John. He has continued his writing and in addition has produced and directed for television.

### David Stollery

After playing Marty in the "Spin and Marty" series, David completed his education and traveled to Italy, where he designed furniture. He holds a real estate license, and works as a design engineer. He is married and has no children.

### Roy Williams

Roy continued to work for the Disney organization for many years after the Mickey Mouse Club's demise. He spent some time as a cartoonist at Disneyland and assisted on the traveling pageant "Disney on Parade." He only recently retired, and still contributes to the Disney Studio — working in story development and making plans for a *new* Mickey Mouse Club, which the company hopes to unveil in 1977.

### Jimmie Dodd

Jimmie made personal appearances to support the Mickey Mouse Club throughout its initial run and during its first syndication. He and Ruth Dodd continued to entertain until Jimmie's sudden death in Hawaii in 1964.

# Nancy Abbate

Nancy's motion picture credits since the club include *Love Is Better Than Ever, Artists and Models,* and *The Farmer Takes a Wife.* A cocktail waitress at Caesar's Palace in Las Vegas, Nancy is widowed and has a fifteen-year-old son.

# Don Agrati (Don Grady)

Following the club, Don served an eleven-year stint as one of "My Three Sons." A singer and keyboard specialist who also plays nine other instruments, Don had his first album, "Homegrown," released on the Elektra label in 1974. He is currently recording a second album in the basement studio of his Laguna Beach home and is featured in Max Baer's film, *The Wild McCulloughs*. Don is a bachelor.

# Sherry Allen

In 1966, Sherry was honored as Hollywood Star Deb, and in 1968 she was Hollywood Princess of the Month. Today, she is an actress who specializes in voice characterizations for television cartoons. She is heard on "Super Friends," "Josie and the Pussycats," and "The Partridge Family." Sherry is married to Dr. Richard Van Meter, a physician, and has a one-year-old daughter.

# *Sharon Baird*

Now a veteran of motion pictures and nightclubs, Sharon is active in children's television. She dances and dons a number of animal costumes for Sid and Marty Krofft's "Lidsville," "Pufinstuff," "Sigmund and the Sea Monsters," and is also seen on the "New Zoo Revue," "Land of the Lost," and "Charley and the Owl." A divorcee, Sharon resides in Sherman Oaks.

# *Billie Jean Beanblossom*

Billie Jean danced for about five years after leaving the club, and subsequently taught dancing for another three. She now enjoys family life as the mother of two children and as the wife of Ted Cooper, a senior buyer for Lockheed in Burbank. Billie Jean works as a personal secretary for Valley-Todeco, Inc., in the San Fernando Valley.

# *Bobby Burgess*

For the past thirteen years, Bobby has created and performed dances as a weekly regular on "The Lawrence Welk Show." He has worked in nightclubs in every state but Alaska, and makes numerous concert and fair appearances. In 1971, Bobby married Kristie Floren, the daughter of Lawrence Welk's assistant and accordian virtuoso Myron Floren.

# *Lonnie Burr*

Lonnie Burr has a bachelor's degree from San Fernando Valley State College, a master's from UCLA, and has done work toward a doctorate. His musical comedy credits include *Mack and Mabel, Irma La Douce, West Side Story,* and the National Company of *George M.* In addition, Lonnie has published poetry, won seven literary awards, and served as co-editor of *Quiddity,* a poetry journal. Lonnie now resides in Los Angeles.

# Tommy Cole

Tommy graduated from Hollywood Professional School and Pasadena City College. He played nightclubs in 1962–63, and in 1966 joined The Young Generation and Johnny Mathis to tour the United States and the Orient. Now a makeup man at NBC's Burbank Studio, Tommy has been married since 1968. He lives in Van Nuys, California.

# *Eileen Diamond*

After the club, Eileen made several films and danced in musical comedies starring Howard Keel, Ann Miller, and Martha Raye. She and her husband, conductor-producer Roy Rogosin, are planning a stage version of *The Umbrellas of Cherbourg*. The Rogosins have a four-year-old daughter and are expecting a second child by Christmas, 1975. Eileen and Roy reside in North Hollywood.

# *Mary Espinosa*

Mary has been variously employed as a saleswoman, keypunch operator, and employment interviewer. For the past three years, she has worked for the Family Health Program of Long Beach, California. The busy mother of an eight-year-old son and ten-year-old daughter, Mary still finds time to entertain at a local convalescent home near Long Beach. She is recently divorced.

# Bonnie Lynn Fields

Although her Mouseketeeshirt read "Bonnie," Ms. Fields now prefers to be called Lynn. After the club, she attended business college in Richmond, Indiana. She appeared in the films *Sweet Charity, Funny Girl,* and *Bye Bye Birdie,* and on television's "Dr. Kildare," "Red Skelton," and "The Andy Williams Show." Lynn is presently business manager of Century Leasing and Management Co. in Los Angeles, and her hobbies include ballet, tap dancing, gourmet cooking, and making her own clothes. Lynn is unmarried.

# Annette Funicello

Annette is married to theatrical agent Jack Gilardi. They have three children: Gina (nine), Jack, Jr. (five), and Jason (one year). Annette works professionally only on rare occasions, preferring to devote herself to homemaking and raising her children.

# Darlene Gillespie

Since the Mickey Mouse Club, Darlene has acted on television and in many stage plays in the Los Angeles area. She also studied nursing and became a specialist in cardiac disorders. At present, Darlene has turned to a new entertainment career. Under the name Darlene Valentine, she is a country-western singer, recording for Alva Records. Married to Phil Gammon, an independent gasoline retailer, Darlene has a son, age two, and a daughter, age three and one-half.

# Judy Harriet

After her Mickey Mouse Club days, Judy formed her own night-club act and performed in a variety of television series and films. In 1964, she married Tony Richman. They have two daughters, Lisa (four) and Jenny (two). Although her roles as a housewife and mother have kept her out of show business for several years now, Judy says she still has the urge to perform before a live audience.

# Cheryl Holdridge

Photo by Gene Lester

Cheryl attended high school and college in Los Angeles, making appearances on "My Three Sons," "Bachelor Father," and "Dobie Gillis." In 1970, she married racing Woolworth heir Lance Reventlow. Lance died in 1972. Cheryl now lives in Beverly Hills. She is remarried.

# *Bonni Lou Kern*

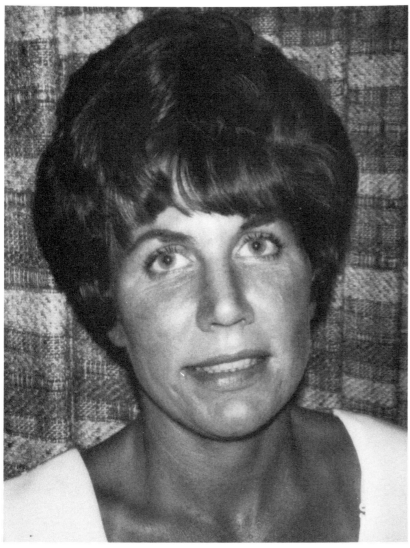

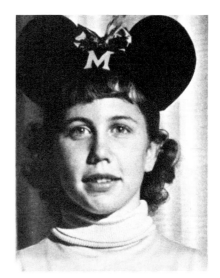

Bonni lost interest in a show business career and instead became a top executive in a business firm. She is married to Harold (Bud) Carr, a driver for United Parcel Service, and they have two children. The Carrs live in Alhambra, California, where they enjoy camping trips and handcrafts such as macramé and making terrariums.

# Carl "Cubby" O'Brien

The former Meesketeer further developed his talent as a drummer, and became a regular orchestra member on "The Carol Burnett Show." He was a studio musician for many years and served as a musical director for the stage hit, *Hair*. Cubby now tours and records with Karen and Richard Carpenter—and still dons his mouse ears as part of their act. Cubby and his wife Marilyn have a five-year-old daughter.

# Karen Pendleton

Karen studied sociology at California State University, Northridge, and is currently employed by Prudential Life Insurance Co. in Los Angeles. She married her high school sweetheart Mike DeLauer in 1970, and is now the mother of a one-year-old girl. Although Karen has set aside show business for the present, she continues to dance whenever she can.

# *Paul Petersen*

A ''Donna Reed Show'' cast member for eight years, Paul returned to the Disney Studio to act in *The Happiest Millionaire*. He has since forsaken an acting career in favor of writing. He has had ten books published, including *High Performance Driving* and *The Smugglers*. Paul lives with his wife Hallie in Westport, Connecticut, where they have a five-month-old son Brian.

# *Lynn Ready*

Lynn made appearances on "Ozzie and Harriet," and in *My Fair Lady,*
*Bye Bye Birdie,* and *The Collector.* He is single, living in Canoga Park,
California, and is presently recording an album of original songs.

# Mary Sartori

Mary attended Pasadena City College and continued her dancing. She made a TV series, "Sheriff of Cochise," and then married Lee Celano, a wholesale meat dealer, in 1962. They have two boys, one seven and the other eleven. The Celanos reside in Glendale, California.

# Bronson Scott

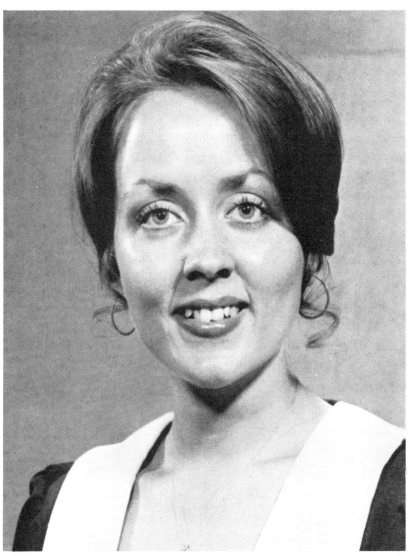

Bronson has a bachelor's degree in Business Administration (Marketing-Advertising), and while in school she worked in photography, fashion modeling, performed for schools, hospitals, and benefits. She is married to Charles Schott and has recently left a successful business career to become a full-time housewife. As yet, she has no children.

# *Margene Storey*

Margene graduated from high school, junior college, and beauty college. She worked for six years as a hair stylist in Salinas, California, before taking her present position as an automobile salesperson. Margene is divorced and has two children.

# Doreen Tracey

*Photo by Matt Kramer*

Doreen Tracey performed with the Andressi Brothers in Las Vegas and toured Viet Nam with the USO. She made guest appearances on "Day in Court," "The Donna Reed Show," and "My Three Sons." Divorced and the mother of one child, Doreen presently does promotional work for DiscreetRecords in Hollywood. This picture was taken when Doreen won first place in the first Woman's Weightlifting Tournament (Sept. 6, 1975).

M-I-C

And so, the Mickey Mouse Club lives—on the air·and in the lives of the people who made it. There are certain Mouseketeers, however, whose whereabouts are a mystery. The studio has been unable to contact:

Dickie Dodd
John Lee Johann
Charley Laney
Larry Larsen
Ronnie Steiner
Mark Sutherland
Don Underhill

An open invitation to these seven missing mice: should you read this, get in touch.

*See you real soon!*

K-E-Y

*Why? Because we like you!*

M-O-U-S-E

This scrapbook is dedicated to Jimmie Dodd
(1910 –1964) and to Mouseketeers everywhere.